LANDSCAPES

Photographs of Western Australia by Christian Fletcher

Published by

Christian Fletcher Photo Images

P.O. Box 137, Dunsborough, WA 6281

Telephone (08) 9759 1555

www.christianfletcher.com.au

Designed and wholly produced in Australia

ISBN 0–9750771–0–4 (Paper Back)

ISBN 0–9750771–1–2 (Hard Back)

Printed by

Scott Print

40 Short Street, Perth, WA 6000

LANDSCAPES

Photographs of Western Australia by Christian Fletcher

"Molly", Eagle Bay

Thanks to:

Jenny Norton, Michael & Alison Fletcher, Mike Scott, Ted Leach, Julie Mounfield, Colin Seth, Bernie Rusterholz and staff at Scott Print, Paul Maietta and staff at Fitzgerald Photo Lab, Matt Galligan at PRA, Wendy Paine at Planet Graphics, and all those who have helped with this book. Thanks also to Mike and Rob at The Blue Wren, Kathie Fletcher, James Stati, Leanne Taylor, Robyn Ramsden, Trish Allison and Donna Frimston for being part of the team, and last but not least, Fuji the wonderdog.

Photography for me is a lifestyle choice. When I started out all those years ago in a makeshift darkroom, I never thought I'd end up working on a second book. My goal during the early years was to sell some photographs to cover the rent. Having my own galleries wasn't even considered. In the first six years I established a business taking wedding and portrait photos. Six years of "Hell". I finally gave up photography and left on an extended holiday around Australia. Little did I know that I would soon discover the inspiration I needed to carry on and specialize in landscape photography.

Taking photographs is like opening presents on your birthday. You never know what to expect and it's always exciting. Sometimes they're fantastic and other times you wonder why you bothered pushing the shutter. I never lose that feeling of anticipation. Getting the developed films back is the drug that keeps me going and I will always be addicted. Showing them in the galleries is my therapy.

Photographing landscapes over the past six years has given me an appreciation of our natural environment. I have seen some beautiful places bathed in beautiful light and been left in awe. How anyone can ignore their responsibility to this planet and it's treasures still amazes me. I hope this book will inspire you to conserve what we have today for future generations.

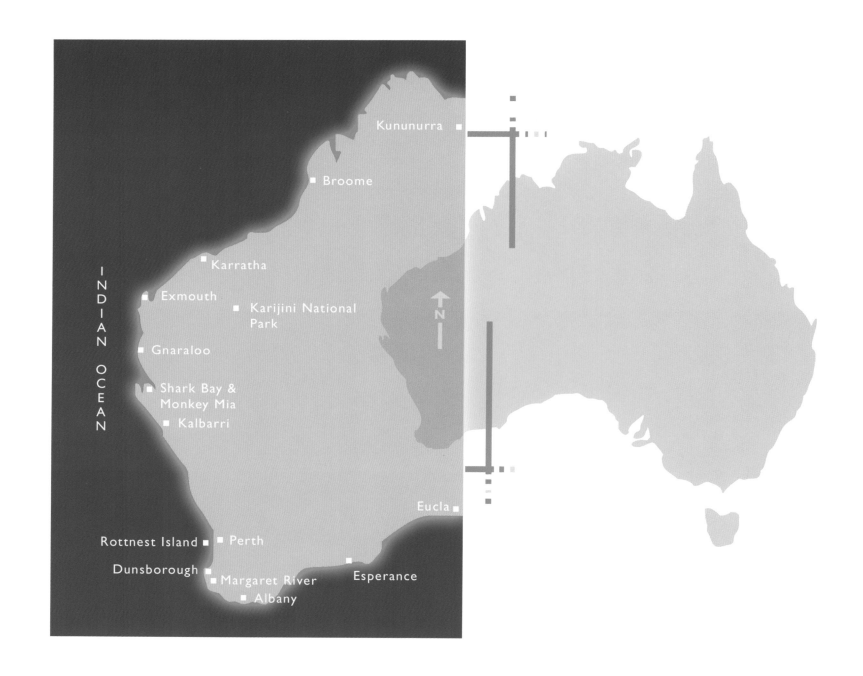

INDIAN OCEAN

Kununurra ■

■ Broome

■ Karratha

■ Exmouth

■ Karijini National Park

■ Gnaraloo

■ Shark Bay & Monkey Mia

■ Kalbarri

Eucla ■

Rottnest Island ■ ■ Perth

Dunsborough ■

■ Margaret River

Esperance

■ Albany

3 Mile Camp, Gnaraloo

Hay Bales, Wilyabrup

Cape Naturaliste is one of my favourite places to photograph. It has a certain mystery. It is one of the places I have photographed which gives me a sense of isolation. This is strange considering it is only 12km's from Dunsborough and popular with surfers and bush walkers. I have had many late afternoons out there and the feeling is alway the same. Walking along the coast in fading light, often shrouded in sea mist, it is possible to imagine being the only person alive.

The coastline between Carnarvon and Exmouth has some of Australia's best beaches. The waters are alive with every fish imaginable. Gnaraloo is one of the accessable places and is popular with surfers and fishermen. On this particular trip I wanted to get some magic light, some cloud, anything other than straight blue sky. Unfortunately it is almost always sunny so it wasn't to be. This photograph is one of my most popular and I almost missed it. I had to be convinced to take the shot. The starfish really was there, I didn't pull a plastic one out of my pocket as someone had suggested. That is what Gnaraloo is like, unbelievable.

Rottnest Island was one of the most difficult places to shoot. Not because it is'nt beautiful, but because you have to ride your bike everywhere. Here I was, hurtling down the path to Longreach Bay, camera and tripod in hand on a bike with one brake. This image is a typical scene summing up the experience that is "Rotto". My bike is second from the right.

The sand dunes at Injidup are constantly on the move. I have heard of a time when the point was completely vegetated but I only know of it this way. This photo was taken on a very average summer day. I wasn't expecting too much or looking forward to the walk, but determined not to go back empty handed. This scene appeared and I took a shot. I'm glad I did.

40   "Shotover", Monkey Mia

Eastern Bluff, Monkey Mia

Yungarra Estate, Dunsborough

I took this photo a few years ago and I still love it today. On waking I noticed the sky in the east to be very overcast. I thought there could be a chance for some nice light if I could get a break in the clouds. Whilst loading my gear into the car the sky began to fill with colour... "Panic stations" Heading for the first place I thought of, I stopped and jumped out of the car. Having to clamber over a locked gate added to my stress. I didn't want to lose this light. I quickly set up the camera and took one 30 second exposure. Satisfied I had the shot I packed up and drove home. All up I was there for about five minutes. I was lucky to be in the right place at the right time. You can visit a location many times but if it's not happening on the day, forget it.

The greatest thing about photography is that it is only restricted by your imagination. The ability to see shapes or patterns in an object, to have a vision of something that could be, is what all photographers wish to have and with time can develop. This series of three images were taken early one morning. Fuji, our dog, needed a walk, and despite being extremely hung over, I managed to roll out of bed and get moving. I had the close-up on and walked slowly across the cool sand of the beach, head bowed and pounding. Fuji was in total contrast, happy, energetic and having fun. Who said photography was easy.

54   Winter Stream, Millbrook Farm, Yallingup

One of my all time favourite and most popular images, also the result of pure luck. I never wait for long periods of time for the light to be "just right", if it's not happening when I'm there I move on. By photographing most days I will get lucky more often. On this particular morning I drove to the boat ramp to check the horizon, I normally do this to see if there will be any breaks in the clouds to get some magic light ... and there it was laid out in front of me. I set up the camera, took one shot and left. People say you should at least take a couple of shots or bracket your exposures but I never have. I take one and move on. By doing this you are taught to get it right the first time, taking more care with your composition and exposure.

Karijini National Park in the Hamersley Ranges is probably the most spectacular place in Western Australia. It is amazing that more people don't know where it is. I always have a desire to go back there as it has so much to offer. A trip to Karijini is not an easy one and is definately out if you desire luxury accomodation and room service. For this reason it has remained a relative secret to most Australians and has not been spoilt by over use. Photographing in the gorges has its challenges but their magnificence makes the effort worthwhile. As always shooting in the early morning or late afternoon will help make a photograph better. This image was taken late in the afternoon.

66   Thomson Bay, Rottnest Island

Bathurst Lighthouse, Rottnest Island

Emma Gorge, Kimberley

Hellfire Bay, Cape Le Grand National Park, Esperance

84   The Bell Tower, Perth

Blue Lagoon, Esperance

Honeycombes, Wilyabrup

Karri Valley, Pemberton

Sand Patterns, Foul Bay, Cape Leeuwin

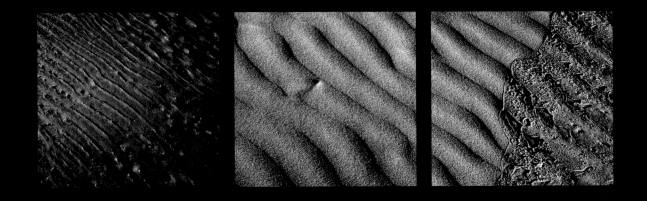

Ocean Beach, Denmark

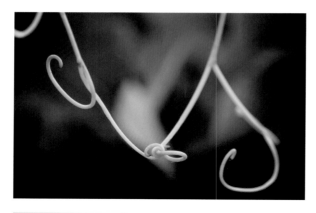

Quindalup Boat Ramp, Geographe Bay

What a difference a day makes. Compare this shot to the front cover. It is amazing how light can be affected by clouds and the atmosphere as this photograph shows. The change in weather and season can dramatically alter the mood of a photograph and in turn influence the shape and form of the landscape.

Amberley Estate, Yallingup

Wilson Inlet, Denmark

Eastern Bluff, Monkey Mia

138   Five Rivers Lookout, Bastion Range, Wyndham

146   Boab Trees, Kununurra, Kimberley

The images featured in this book are all available as fine art photographic prints.

For Christian's gallery information and on-line web site visit:
www.christianfletcher.com.au

INDEX

INDEX

For the last three years my camera of choice has been the FujiGX617. I only use one lens, a 90 mm. I also use a Bronica SQAI with lenses ranging from 50mm to 150mm and a Cannon D60. The only filter I use is a polariser, which is permanently corroded to the lens, and Fuji Velvia film. I have a heavy duty Manfrotto tripod for building my muscles and use a Lowe Pro pack to avoid trips to the physio. All of it is getting tired, but like me, "getting better with age", and the old saying is still relevant, "it's not what you've got, it's how you use it"!